a youth

# CRASH COURSE

Everything
you need to
know, from
adolescence
to zits

# a youth ministry

CRASH COURSE

Everything you need to know, from adolescence to zits

Rick Bundschuh and E.G. Von Trutzschler

## Youth Specialties

ZondervanPublishingHouse
*Grand Rapids, Michigan*
*A Division of HarperCollinsPublishers*

*A Youth Ministry Crash Course: Everything you need to know, from adolescence to zits*

© 1996 by Youth Specialties, Inc.

Youth Specialties Books, 300 S. Pierce St., El Cajon, CA 92020, are published by Zondervan Publishing House, 5300 Patterson Ave. S.E., Grand Rapids, MI 49530.

**Library of Congress Cataloging-in-Publication Data**

Bundschuh, Rick, 1951-
    A youth ministry crash course : everything you need to know, from adolescence to zits \ Rick Bundschuh and E.G. Von Trutzschler.
      p.  cm.
    ISBN 0-310-21528-5
    1. Church work with youth—United States—Handbooks, manuals, etc. 2. Christian education of young people—United States—Handbooks, manuals, etc. I. Von Trutzschler, E.G. II. Title.
BV4447.B78   1996
259'.23—dc21                           96-45054
                                                    CIP

*Edited by Vicki Newby and Tim McLaughlin*
*Cover and interior design by Rogers Design & Associates*
*Illustrations by Rick Bundschuh*

*Printed in the United States of America*

99 00 02 03 04 05 06/ /14 13 12 11 10 9 8 7 6 5

For "Pooch" Claytor and Jennie Trask. Thanks for all you do.

# Contents

# Experience is a good teacher.

Regardless of the college degrees they hold, youth workers begin their real education at the youth-room door.

As veteran youth workers (we have nearly 70 years of full-time youth work between the two of us), we've seen and learned plenty. We've worked in small, struggling churches as well as big ones. We've worked with church kids and with street kids. We've survived the twists and turns of church politics. We've seen kids in our groups grow into adulthood with a flourishing faith. And we've seen kids in our groups turn their backs on God, in spite of our best efforts.

Our students have taught us as much about God's love and grace as we've taught them. We're convinced that an investment in teenagers is one of the best uses of time, energy, and resources a church can make.

# The fountain of youth.

Some youth workers seem to have found the fountain of youth. Their effectiveness spreads across a number of generations. (We like to think that we're among those—despite the fact that one of us is an aging baby boomer and the other a senior citizen.) The secret isn't in bottled water or Gray Be Gone hair coloring, but rather in practical principles of youth work consistently practiced. A lot has changed in the last thirty years—but there's also a lot of wisdom that applies as much today as it did thirty years ago. It's these unchanging principles and tips that make up the lion's share of this book.

If you're fairly new to youth ministry, this short volume will be a treasury of helpful ideas for you—and now and then just may save you from learning the hard way.

Of course, an alert and seasoned youth worker will already have arrived at these youth worker laws intuitively. If you're such a youth worker, *A Youth Ministry Crash Course* will be a joyful affirmation that your impulses are right on target—and a convenient, spirited way to bring your volunteers up to speed, too.

As we dredged up principles and ideas from our years of youth ministry, we thought again of our great debt to those men and women who stood beside us, cleaned up after us, drove the bus for us, spent time with the kids when we couldn't or wouldn't, defended us, stayed up all night with us, gave up their vacations to be camp counselors for us, befriended us when no other adults wanted to be associated with us—and seldom got the recognition or respect they deserved because they were merely "volunteer youth staff." It's to them (and their beloved rubber chickens) we dedicate this book.

# Accolades

If you need a lot of these, you may want to forget about youth work altogether. The rewards are mostly of a heaven variety.

The job is misunderstood by many. Some think you're not really working, but just having fun all the time. (These are the same people who think you actually enjoy staying up all night at a lock-in.)

Then there's the popularity paradox. If the kids like you, it makes the parents nervous. If the parents like you, it makes the kids nervous. If everyone likes you, it makes the pastor nervous.

The church won't remember all the youth events that went right, but they'll never let you forget the time when a couple of goofballs plugged the toilet with paper towels and the ensuing overflow flooded the pastor's study.

Ninety-nine out of a hundred kids won't acknowledge all the work and energy you put in on the job. But a day will come, years later, when you'll get a note from an adult with a vaguely familiar name, that says you meant the world to her during her teen years. Most veterans frame these; sometimes these get you through the day. (See Files.)

# Addresses

The most important things to collect are the addresses, phone numbers, birth dates, and grades of your kids—including the visitors. Keep them up to date, too. It's a good idea to create phone and mailing lists to give to your kids at least twice a year. Otherwise they'll always be calling you to get the number of some kid. (See Newcomers.)

# Adolescence

The time of life when kids enter a thick fog. They don't know where they're going and can't tell where they've been—but wherever they're going, they usually do it full speed ahead. It's your job to be a fog horn, to keep them from piling up on the rocks until the fog lifts and they exit adolescence.

# Advertising

You need to make kids aware of the youth group and its programs. Blimps, Elvis impersonators, and similar forms of blatant advertising only drive kids away. So try some subtle ways to let it be known that your group is doing great stuff.

➤ **T-shirts** can build *esprit de corp* and call attention to your group at the same time.

➤ **Book covers** with info about your church—or even the gospel—work great at the beginning of school when kids are required to cover their books. See pages 85–86 for a resource. The cost is low.

➤ **Mail-outs** are a must. Tons of terrific clip art is available to spruce those babies up. Be sure to make address-collecting a top priority.

➤ Be on the lookout for **new technology** that can help

publicize your group. You may want to start a home page on the Internet featuring your group's activities.

➢ **Photo boards** hung in the church halls quietly chronicle all the great stuff your group does.
(See Linking.)

## Age Has Priority

FRONT SEAT, PLEASE!

This is a simple rule you can use to decide who gets to ride in the front seat, which kids have to sleep in the mildewed tent, who gets the top bunk, and countless other things that kids fight and bicker about. Whoever is oldest (right down to minutes or seconds of birth if you have twins) gets first choice.

We admit that Age Has Priority is not nearly as good a solution as Christian Love. But Christian Love may be as scarce as hen's teeth in some groups. If this is your case, this little rule works wonders. The younger kids hate the rule, but it gives them something to look forward to. They can hardly wait to get old enough to use it on the runts.

## Attention Spans

A kid has a kid's attention span. The younger the kid, the shorter the attention span—unless they're doing something cool, like tormenting ants. Be conscious of your group's attention span when preparing a lesson or activity. Just because you have an hour to fill doesn't mean you'll have your gang's attention for that long.

## Be Yourself

Youth-working dorks who try hard to be cool are still dorks. If God made you a dork, relax and be a lovable dork. Kids don't need you to look cool or spew slang. Kids will respect any adult who loves them, cares about them, and takes time for them—even if they look dopey and like awful music.

## Bibles

You may be amazed at how many kids don't bring Bibles to a Bible study. So have extras lying around. If lots of new kids are coming to your program, make sure to have easy-to-read, freebie Bibles they can take home with them.

## Bigger and Better

Yes, you want to attract new kids into the youth group. But watch out that you don't fall into the bigger-and-better trap. Kids have a voracious appetite and may adopt a Can You Top This? attitude. Before long you'll have gone from a few simple crowd breakers to alligator wrestling. Different is a better (and easier) way to go than bigger and better.

# Birthdays

Everyone, whether they admit it or not, likes to have the ol' birthday acknowledged. Find out the dates of your students' birthdays and mark them on your calendar. Buy or make a bunch of cards, then send each teen a short birthday greeting at the appropriate time.

At meetings, haul the birthday kids to the front and give them each a Twinkie with a candle in it as a token cake.

Or have a One-Minute Birthday Party. Put a hat on the birthday girl and give her a cupcake and candle. Present a simple gift. Throw confetti and streamers, make a lot of noise, and sing the birthday song for the grand finale. When sixty seconds are up, snatch everything away from her—even the cupcake and gift—and have her sit down. To show that you're not *completely* heartless, toss the cupcake back. Recycle the stuff for the next birthday.

# Brainwashing

A brainwashing session is simply a short meeting before an event, camp, or other significant activity when you explain the rules of behavior. Tell your group all the do's and don'ts, your expectations, how far it is between potty stops, and any other details they'll need to know. A well-thought-out brainwash means you don't have to repeat the same things over and over, and it saves you from making up rules on the run. (See Rules.)

# Calendars

You too can seem really organized. Impress your friends and coworkers. Buy a three-year planning calendar and do just that—plan. Find out when school starts and ends for summer and spring break. Reserve camp sites well into the future. Note youth convention dates in Hawaii. Dream.

# Camps and Retreats

Schedule several camps or retreats every year. A lot more can be accomplished away from the normal everyday routine. If you plan it right, a camp or retreat can be a spiritual hot-house for teens. See pages 85–86 for retreat-planning resources.

# Cancellations

A reliable rule of thumb in youth work is NEVER CANCEL. Canceling punishes the kids who've made plans to attend and sends them the message that you don't care about them. When we've had to cancel, it was usually because we blew it somewhere along the line in planning, publicity, or scheduling.

On the other hand, a cancellation can work if it's built into the activity as a possibility. For example, include a caveat like "In the event of alien invasion or really bad rain, this camping trip will be canceled."

# Case the Joint

If it's at all possible, check out the site where you'll take your kids well in advance. This way you seem way smarter than your students because you know where the bathrooms are, which drinking fountains work, where kids who want to make out are likely to head so you can be there waiting for them, etc. (See Control.)

# Chemistry

Chemistry is the result of mixing various personalities together. Every youth group has its own chemistry, and even that chemistry changes from year to year, or even meeting to meeting, depending on the combination of kids present. If last year's group was lively, fun, dynamic, and this year the kids sit around staring at their navels, it may have a lot to do with chemistry. If the chemistry is on the sluggish side, try to get new kids into the program to stir up the present crew.

# Choosing Teams

Games happen. When teams are chosen, the social outcast or new kid often gets picked last. Remedy this with creative ways to get kids into teams or groups without hurt feelings:

➢ Line the boys up, tallest to shortest—and do the same with the girls. Count them off into the number of teams you need. This way size and stature will be fairly even so one team doesn't mow down another.

➢ Stick tape of various colors on the backs of kids. (Be as random or as deliberate as the game and your sense of fairness requires.) Each color is a team.

➤ Use games such as Clumps or Barnyard that automatically put kids into groups. See pages 85–86 for game resources. (See Games, Points.)

# Church Coffee Pot

Typical of the kind of thing that *really* matters to some churches (as opposed to the doctrine of the Trinity, the Great Commission, etc.). Know ahead of time how sacred the church coffee pot is before you use it as a soda dispenser at the youth group's Back to School party. (See Moving On.)

# Church Vehicles

Many churches and youth organizations have buses or vans. Most states require a special license to drive the vehicle.

So never get that license. If you do, you'll be drafted any time a bus is needed for anything. After all, they hired you to run around inside the bus and be with kids, not to drive the thing.

Besides, using a church-owned vehicle often requires a ton of forms and red tape. You may find it easier to buy a van of your own to haul kids. It just may save you a lot of hassle. (See Driving.)

# Cliques

The plague of many youth groups is tight, unfriendly clusters of kids who are cool in their own eyes. Counter their exclusive coolness with devices that force kids to interact with those outside themselves and their coolness cliques—like assigning seats, or intentionally separating those in cliques during games. They'll moan and whine; you just smile and say (sweetly), "Tough luck!"

An example of randomly seating kids: as students enter the room, hand each a colored strip (of paper, fabric, etc.), and immediately ask kids to put their names on the strips. (This keeps kids from trading with other kids once they figure out what's going on.) Then break into groups according to the color of the strips. (See Xenophobia.)

# Comfort Zones

One of the best things you can do for your kids is to get them out of their comfort zones and into tough real-life situations that aren't easy for them. Mission trips, old folks homes, institutions for the retarded, soup kitchens, and rescue missions are all likely to stretch kids. A visit to a mortuary, a Synagogue, or even another youth group can give you a lot of teachable moments. (See Missions.)

# Communication

Take advantage of the magic that technology has done for communication. Get a direct phone line to your youth office and hook up an answering machine so kids can hear your announcements of upcoming events and leave their own messages for you. Ask your group's hacker to create a home page. Get online yourself in order to e-mail your kids individually or with whole-group messages.

# Competition

Kids love competition, despite the fact that the idea of competition goes in and out of style according to what's politically correct at the moment. Like anything else, competition can get out of hand and become hurtful or mean-spirited. It can bring out poor sportsmanship and reveal those who can't stand to lose.

On the other hand, a bit of competition can be fun, healthy, and energizing. Competition can be designed on different levels so that everyone has an equal chance to excel. Suppose, for instance, you have several teams competing in a camp setting. Give the same amount of points to the team that builds the best raft out of used milk cartons and duck tape as you give to the team that rows across the lake fastest. This way, both your engineers *and* your athletes are affirmed.

# Confidentiality

Kids will tell you lots of stuff in confidence—as long as you keep the information confidential. Once you blab, you won't be trusted. Kids instinctively avoid a rat. Keep confidences unless the health of the person involved (or someone else) is threatened. And in those cases, tell them why you cannot keep their confidences.

Many states carry laws that *require* you to take specific action if you're made aware of certain problems, and in fact hold you criminally liable if you *don't* inform authorities. For example, you may be required to report information about suspected child abuse to the police. Failure to do so can put you in grave legal jeopardy. Be sure you know your state laws about such matters. (See Counseling.)

# Control

Kids need and want control that authority brings, even if they push the rules and act like they want raw anarchy. One of a youth worker's prime duties is to keep things from spinning out of control. Avoid doing anything that tosses control to a kid. Don't walk out of a classroom or off the stage during a meeting—this only creates a vacuum that your crazier students will be happy to fill. Never hand the junior high group a bucket of paint and a few brushes, and then leave for an appointment. Don't let them count the offering by themselves. (See Case the Joint.)

# Costume Boxes

If you ever wished you had a pair of x-ray glasses, a nice fright wig, and a long hillbilly beard to wear at a youth meeting, you'll see the wisdom of a costume box. You can stock your costume box inexpensively by hitting the after-Halloween sales—you'll pay next to nothing for makeup, masks, and other costume goodies. (See Pencil Box, Prop Box.)

# Counseling

Men should counsel boys, women should counsel girls. If you *must* counsel a teenager of the opposite sex, insist that an adult helper of that gender be with you, or at least within eyeshot if not earshot. Guidelines like these will save you from problems later on.

If stuff comes out during counseling that's beyond your ability to handle, *always* refer—to your supervising pastor or an elder, or to a therapist or other outside professional. (See Confidentiality, Crisis.)

# Creativity

Most creative people are merely thieves. They see a good idea, borrow part of it, tweak it, repaint it, and make it brand new. It's a skill anyone can develop. Observe what others are doing, then modify their ideas to suit your group's needs.

# Crisis

Once in a while—but regularly, if you spend any time at all in youth ministry—you are called into a genuine crisis: a kid in serious legal trouble, a suicide attempt, a death in the family, physical or sexual abuse. Make sure you know—or at least have the numbers of—resource people you can call right away to help handle the situation correctly. Make a copy of your resource-people list for your office, and keep one at home in case you're there when something big hits the fan.

# Cross-Pollination

Hang out now and then with other youth workers in your area and stea—we mean, *recycle* their good ideas. Occasionally join two or three or four of your youth groups for an event. Compare rubber chicken collections.

# Curricula

Most churches and youth ministry organizations want you to use curriculum—sometimes, *their* curriculum. Steal all the great ideas you can from curriculum, but don't be chained to it. You know your kids better than some editor working away in a cubical somewhere. Change it to suit your group, and chuck what doesn't fly.

# Dead Horses

Proverbial warnings against beating a dead horse are particularly true in youth work. Don't let yourself be saddled with a program that's a loser or isn't going anywhere. If you try something new and it becomes unpopular, pull the plug—then see if you can figure out where it went wrong. Some experimentation is fine. The idea may be good, but your group's chemistry or the timing may not be right. (See Dud.)

# Disabilities

A teenager with a disability is one of the best things that can happen to a youth group. Selfishness just drains away, and that young person can bring an attractive chemistry to the group. (See Ugly Duckling.)

# Discipline

Working with kids means that you'll have to be a disciplinarian now and then. You can do it the right way, or you can shoot

23

yourself in the foot. Here's what we've found makes for appropriate and effective discipline:

➢ Discipline away from the crowd. Don't humiliate a kid by correcting her in front of peers.

➢ Use enough discipline to do the job—as much as necessary, as little as possible.

➢ Relate the discipline to the crime, if possible. The kid who's caught writing on the bathroom wall should deep clean the whole bathroom as punishment.

➢ Don't punish the group for the crime of an individual. (See Rules.)

# Discouragement

Youth work isn't always fun. There are times when quitting seems like the best idea you've had for a long, long time. There are times you'll feel absolutely alone, unappreciated, and sniped at—when even the thought of a well-placed whoopee cushion under the church pianist doesn't make you smile. This is where commitment comes in. Hang in there. The feeling is normal. It will pass.

# Disturbances

Every once in a while something or someone will disrupt your meeting or activity: the escapee from the toddler department playing peek-a-boo with your class through an open door...the giant, winged beastie attracted to the spotlights...the car

alarm in the parking lot. The best tack in such circumstances is to acknowledge and deal with the disturbance rather than trying to pretend it isn't happening—everyone knows it is.

# Doors

One of your jobs is to open the doors in students' minds and hearts.

The front door is the one everyone uses, so kids often keep it well guarded. The back door, on the other hand, is the one friends and family use.

So cultivate the skill of using the back door rather than the front door. It's better to walk through the open doorways of a student's personal interests, desire for adventure, involvement in sports, or sense of humor than to pound away on a locked door.

# Double-Checking

Always confirm (and reconfirm) speakers, music guests, reservations, and so on. You can avoid a lot of unpleasant surprises this way.

# Driving

Driving kids comes with youth-work territory. The "message" that kids remember is more likely your chat on the way to camp than the Sunday-morning lesson you planned for all week. Driving time can be productive if you use it. Get to know kids, play road games, be alert for discussions that you can use for off-the-cuff teaching. Just keep your eyes on the road. (See Church Vehicles.)

# Duds

Everyone has had a meeting or activity that was a dud—all promise and no explosion. Kids know when a program or meeting flops. You may be forgiven for one here or there, but a series of them spells trouble.

Kids vote with their feet. Even one dud has an effect that takes hard work and diligence the next time to overcome. (See Dead Horse.)

# Elders' Kids

Never neglect working with the kids of the pastor or elders—even if they're obnoxious. Right or wrong, church leaders inevitably assess the strengths and weaknesses of your ministry by the responses of their own kids. Of course, their kids will always be the most spiritual, the most cooperative, and the friendliest. And the stork brings babies.

# Emergency Kits

Once in a while everything goes wrong. The guest speaker doesn't show. The bus breaks down, stranding you with thirty hyper kids. The copy machine chews up everything you put into it. You wake up Sunday morning with dysentery.

   For these situations you need a ready-made meeting, talk, or quiver of games that need little or no preparation. Better yet, put your emergency kit in a brightly labeled box where other staff can find it—in case your sudden absence is the emergency.

# Emotions

Adolescents tend to be very emotional. A shrewd youth worker can use that tendency to get the group worked up over just about anything. Emotions quickly pass and are poor foundations on which to build big decisions—so be wary about how strongly you play on kids' emotions.

## Evaluations

Every so often evaluate your program, your goals, and your activities to be sure you're not spinning your wheels. Make it a team evaluation, a questionnaire for the kids, or an evaluation with a few key staff members.

## Evangelism

The best method of evangelism, we've found, is personal and relational. Create situations where kids make intellectual or willful— not just emotional— commitments to Christ. Strive for light, not heat.

# Families

Like it or not, a youth worker's family must march to the beat of a different drummer. Youth workers work with youth, so they must be available when youths are available. During the school year this usually means afternoons, evenings, and weekends—the very times, unfortunately, when so-called normal families are most often together.

To meet the needs of your family, then, take mornings off. Or make Monday and Tuesday your "weekend." Do whatever creative scheduling it takes for you to stay connected with your family, or for you to have a life outside of youth ministry.

# Files

Keep a file full of curious, intriguing, or outlandish stories that you can use during your Bible studies. Clip them from newspapers and magazines. Photocopy them from books.

And keep a file of encouraging nice letters you have received about the impact of your ministry. Drag them out on those days when you'd rather be a crash test dummy than a youth worker. You'll feel much better after reading them. (See Accolades.)

# Food

Having food around after a meeting ensures kids will not run off too quickly. They'll stay and interact with each other. The quality of the munchies doesn't have to be high; the mere presence of edibles works.

When running camps or retreats, cut off your snack bar at least an hour before your mealtime. Kids, being kids, will fill up on junk and then toss out good food at meals.

Also at camps and events, limit how much sugar you provide for kids. Some go sonic on a sugar rush.

If you want your kids to eat, know their favorite foods. Pizza, hamburgers, sloppy joes, tacos, spaghetti, and grilled cheese sandwiches are more likely to find their way into adolescent digestive systems than grilled liver.

# Friends

A teen's friends are his conscience. To be cool in the eyes of friends is worth more than just about anything else. And, yes—if their friends all jumped over a cliff, your students would probably be jumping off right behind them (although they'd say they were pushed).

The friends of any kid in your group are all realistic contacts for ministry. Kids will tell their friends about stuff they like. It's the best formula for growth.

# Fundraising

Many churches need their students to pitch in and help fund their own programs. While this is fair enough, it's easy for fundraising events to become all-consuming for you and the kids—and ultimately obnoxious to the rest of the congregational flock, who too easily feel fleeced when you're constantly soliciting funds from them.

Reserve fundraising activities for special occasions. Make sure the kids are willing partners. Plan and promote your event

and intended financial goal.

A car wash is a typical fundraiser for youth groups, probably because putting a water hose in a kid's hands is safer than buckets of paint or riding lawn mowers—plus the car wash usually turns into a friend wash within the first fifteen minutes, which is fun.

With a little imagination you can come up with other clever and even lucrative ways to help fund your program. See pages 85–86 for fundraising resources.

# Games

For kids, games are the fun part of the equation. A quality game is fast-paced and organized, involves the kids, provides an escape valve for energy, and helps kids have a great time. See pages 85–86 for game resources.

A few tips that will help make your games run smoothly:
➤ Give clear, simple rules and boundaries. Make sure everyone understands them before you begin. Draw a diagram if it helps.
➤ Make sure teams are well identified. Rolls of plastic surveyor's tape in day-glo colors don't cost much at a hardware store; use the tape as headbands or armbands to distinguish teams.
➤ Don't be stingy with points.
➤ Anticipate cheating. In the heat of competition, even saints' halos can become tarnished. Figure out how kids might cheat or cut corners—then figure out how to diminish those possibilities.
➤ Make sure everyone can hear your signals or instructions. It's always a drag when some kid is still hiding hours after everyone else has gone home.
(See Choosing Teams, Points.)

# Gross Stuff

Never under estimate a junior higher's capacity to enjoy gross stuff. Boys revel in it. Need to get attention

quickly? A descent into the realm of the gross always does the trick.

# Guys (i.e, males)

This may be the depth of politically incorrectness, but it's always worked for us: design and orient your ministry toward guys.

Here's why. Most girls make guys their hobby. The hobby of most guys is sports or other activities. Therefore, if you attract guys, you'll attract girls. Unfortunately, the inverse of this principle doesn't work: attracting girls to your youth group doesn't tend to attract guys, particularly the kind of guys you may want for your group's core.

So for each event, meeting, and activity, ask yourself, "Would most guys go for this?" If the answer is yes, you can be sure your meetings will be interesting to both guys *and* girls.

# Horn Tooting

Don't be afraid to toot your own horn. A youth worker can't afford to be modest or quiet. If you're doing something, let it be known.

Horn tooting can be subtle: Take your pastor or a key leader out for lunch to share what's been happening with your ministry. It can be overt—glorify your group's accomplishments in the church periodicals, hang photo posters in the hall, have group members give testimonies during the church service.

Use any method you can to let others know about the good stuff God is doing with, through, and to your group.

# Hot Spots

These are places where teens in your community tend to congregate—so it stands to reason that these are also great places to get to know kids and for them to see who you are.

Don't show up with your "turn-or-burn" placards, but engage kids in discussions and make contacts. In many cities you can still get on school campuses during lunch. Not only will you have a hot spot but a captive audience as well.

## Information

You're planning the Great Youth Event of the Decade: The Poisonous Rattlesnake Knot-Tying Contest. You know what your intentions are, you know it's safe. But do Mom and Dad? Communicate in writing all the information that parents need in order to feel confident and comfortable with your event. Spell out the who, what, where, why, when, and how much of each activity.

Make sure kids know what to bring and what to expect. Don't make your promotional pieces so cool or clever that you forget to point out the essentials.

Be honest in your information. If your event is an evangelistic event disguised as a beach party, say so. Otherwise kids feel tricked.

## Inheritance

If you're new on the scene, chances are that you'll have inherited a preexisting youth group. This is great if the kids are great. But what if you inherit a group of slugs—you know, ABC kids: apathetic, bored, closed.

Divide and conquer! Administrate your slugs into their own little program. Spend a minimum amount of time with them. Then go out and round up some normal kids. Become friends and start activities with them. Pretty soon you'll have two programs going. When your healthy program gets large enough, move in the slugs, and then watch how they get moving. (See Cliques, Xenophobia.)

# Interns

Some churches set up special programs for wannabe youth workers. Working for nothing or next to nothing, an intern gets practical, on-the-job experience from working shoulder to shoulder with a seasoned pro.

If you constantly have more work than you can handle—and particularly if you have a supply of Christian college students nearby—see if you can talk your church leadership into hiring an intern.

# Involvement Learning

The more involved students become in the learning process, the more interested they'll be and the more they'll retain.

For example, you could explain to your students the parable of the Good Samaritan—or you could ask them to read it themselves and devise a modern version of the parable for them to pantomime. It doesn't take an Einstein to figure out which one will be more memorable to the kids.

# Job Descriptions

Every hired youth worker needs a job description—that sheet or two that lists what you're expected to do, with the line at the end that states how little you'll be paid for doing it.

It's a good idea for any youth worker, paid or not, to ask for a job description. If the church or organization doesn't have one, write your own job description and get it approved. That way you'll be clear on your exact responsibilities so you can confidently refuse to have the Sunday school superintendent or other well-meaning, overworked staff member pump you dry with additional work.

It's also a good idea to give the church a job description of what you expect from them.

# Jokes

Humor is a direct route to a kid's heart. Most teens love to be silly, play practical jokes, and have a good laugh. But be careful. Don't let kids pick on easy targets. Use practical jokes only with those who try to use them on you. Good-natured bantering can suddenly become carnivorous. Play the referee.

# Junior Highers

Also called middle schoolers. These sixth-to-ninth-graders are

among the most despised of God's creatures. Those who have the special grace to work with them will tell you that this twilight zone between childhood and adulthood is nevertheless a time when great things can happen.

Junior highers are full of insecurity and bravado, but are easy to attract—kind of like lemmings. They're also very teachable. They respond best to high-energy activities and hands-on Bible learning. Junior highers generally aren't mobile—beyond bicycles or skateboards, that is—so they enjoy any chance to leave the house. Many are open to spiritual matters, but caution must be taken not to push junior highers to be more than their age can handle.

# Kick Starters

A kick starter gets your group's attention focused on what you want to accomplish. Use one at the beginning of a lesson to get kids thinking, talking, or playing together toward the purpose you have in mind.

To kick start a lesson on listening to God's voice, for instance, blindfold a student and have her walk barefoot through a mine field of mousetraps. You're the "voice of God," verbally directing her safely through the mine field. If the student listens to you carefully, survival is assured. See pages 85–86 for kick-starting resources.

# Kids

These are the creatures you've chosen to work with. They'll fool you, though, for sometimes they can look and even act like adults. But make no mistake: don't expect them to act, reason, feel, or speak as adults. For better or for worse, they're kids. Both you and they will be better off if you deal with them that way.

## Last to Leave

Someone has to be last to leave the meeting or event site. Guess who gets killed if the place is left like a pigpen, if the toilet has

backed up into the sanctuary, if the pastor's office is left unlocked? You. So be the last to leave—or put the job in the hands of someone very responsible. . . like your mother.

## Lawsuits

The threat of lawsuits has put a damper on many youth programs and frustrated many clever youth workers. While it's true that we must use wisdom in what we do and how we do it, reasonable risk is part of the equation for fun.

Avoid overkill. Parental permission slips for a trip to the corner fast-food joint is probably overkill.

## Leadership

You can't lead anyone where you've never been before. Before you try to teach kids life's lessons, you've got to learn them yourself—by personal experience, not merely by reading about them.

# Linking

You can trigger a lot of excitement and growth by linking activities to each other, in a series. Say, for example, three outdoor trips in two months: after your Journey to the Center of the Earth spelunking trip (any caves within an afternoon's drive of your church?), you could take a mountaineering expedition (to the top of that butte in the adjoining county), followed by an attempt to become the first youth group to reach the North Pole (a cross-country ski trek along your town's snow-packed bike trails). You get the idea.

Use each activity to build interest for the next. Maximize the success of the first activity by showing videos or slides of it at your next event. Promote the next linked event by having publicity material ready to distribute right after the show. Smart youth workers know that all the energy and effort put into a good program can be maximized with good advertising. (See Advertising.)

# Literature Table

A literature table or rack can extend your teaching opportunities or provide information on stuff that could be of interest to specific kids. Collect appropriate literature, and make it available before and after meetings. If it's free, short, and easy to read, you can bet kids will take it home. You might even get a bulk subscription to a youth magazine or two for your kids. See pages 85–86 for some titles.

# Mail

Never underestimate the power of a personal letter. Most kids don't get mail. They'll read anything addressed to them, junk mail or not. They'll frame it and keep it as part of a shrine.

# Mentors

Have a few mentors in your life—people strong in faith and wisdom that you can go to for guidance and counsel. Make yourself accountable to these folks to keep you from becoming a dictator, a prima donna, or a dumbbell.

# Minority Rule

Never allow the minority to govern the majority. If one kid tweaks an ankle on a hike, assign responsible staff to help him back to camp—then proceed as planned with the rest of the group.

**45**

# Missions

Kids love missions that offer challenge, adventure, and personal involvement. A missions trip can change a student's life and perspective. A missions trip, in fact, can do far more for your kids than it does for the people your kids minister to.

# Mole Hills

Learn to distinguish them from mountains. Some youth ministry issues will fade away quickly. Others are of lasting importance. In some circles it's popular to go on the attack, or to make an issue out of every cultural trend that comes along. Stick to stuff that has eternal significance. Teach kids *how* to think rather than *what* to think.

# Momentum

You recognize momentum when things seem to be taking off with your youth group. Nobody announces it—you just sense it. Kids are excited and positive...there's a directional movement by the group, perhaps excitement about missions, or telling others about Christ, or Christian music, cow tipping, or just the youth group as a whole. Whatever it is, when you see momentum starting to roll, drop everything else and get on board. The momentum will eventually end. But while it's going, it's a heck of a ride.

# Motives

Have more than one reason for every meeting and special event you plan. Campouts are for kids to get away and have fun, but campouts are also times when kids can get to know other kids in depth. And campouts can be designed to attract new kids. Create programs that meet your kids' felt needs, but also offer ministry opportunities.

## Moving On

Here are the Youth Worker General's warning signs that indicate that it may be time for you to move on:

➢ The senior minister starts to distance himself from you. He offers no shelter when the lynch mob from the women's ministry wants to hang you for allowing the kids to put Dr. Pepper in the church coffee pot. (See Church Coffee Pot.)

➢ There is little or no communication with leadership; for example, they go to a leadership retreat on Maui and don't tell you about it.

➢ They keep you out of the public eye. You aren't even trusted with announcements.

➢ Leadership shows little or no interest in what's going on in youth ministry. A hundred street kids have become Christians this year, and does anyone up there care?

➢ Your budget is cut—past the marrow. Now you have to pay for everything yourself. You say you already do?

➢ Rumblings and criticism against the youth program are entertained—like when the deacon chairman finally snaps and accuses you of being a communist infiltrator.

➢ You return from vacation and your office has been turned into the tape library.

➢ The rubber chicken has pins in it.

# MTV

Regardless of what you think of it, tune it in from time to time. You'll discover what's going on in the youth culture and hear what your kids are probably listening to. (See Music.)

# Music

Music is important to kids. Don't condemn music you don't like or understand. Expose your kids to all kinds of new Christian music. You'll often find issues in secular music that make great discussion starters. (See MTV.)

# Newcomers

Make an effort to meet and get to know new kids. Obtain names and addresses. Follow up with a personal note thanking each for coming to the youth group.

Develop New Kid Awareness among your outgoing teens, so new kids are greeted and made comfortable. Don't embarrass newcomers on their first visits by calling attention to them in front of the crowd.

# No

A good word to learn and occasionally say, usually emphatically. The secret is knowing *when* to say it, *how* to say it, and *to whom* to say it.

# Non-Christians

They can cause dilemmas. We want them at our meetings, but we don't want them to act like the pagans they are.

Non-Christian kids don't understand church etiquette. They don't know

Christian jargon, they don't know their way around the Bible. If they don't like you, they vote with their feet. They tell you when they're bored, they tell you when your game is dumb. They contribute nothing to the offering plate. Non-Christian kids challenge the pecking order of the church kids. Parents worry about the pagan influence on their offspring.

Worst of all, if the little infidels actually like what's going on, they bring their friends.

If you do a good job reaching out to non-Christians, it may cost you. Many youth workers have been surprised to discover that their church leaders prefer nice, quiet youth groups filled with parishioners' children.

# Numbers

When God founded the church centuries ago, he expected it to grow in numbers. A spiritually healthy youth group will tend to do just that.

Like it or not, your performance will probably be judged by numbers. If you manage to lose half the youth group within the first few months of your ministry, you may as well start packing. Healthy groups attract kids. Numbers are the product of good planning, favorable demographics, and the wise investment of time, resources, and energy. (See Success.)

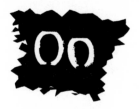

# Office Hours

Life doesn't happen just during office hours. Spend a lot of time in an office and you're efficient. But spend lots of time with kids and you're effective. Most effective youth workers have strange working hours and don't hang around either the office coffee pot or their desks a great deal.

# On Time

In youth work, to be on time means to be early. A good rule of thumb: be there a half-hour before the start of any event. You can set the room up, adjust room temperature, turn the lights on, and scatter the cockroaches before anyone gets there.

Being on time is a good example to the troops. If you're late, you've made a statement that being on time isn't all that important for anyone. (See Time, Timing.)

# Organization

Many otherwise outstanding youth workers nevertheless struggle with organization. Yet a degree of organizational skill is a must to keep things from falling apart.

Before plunging into work, at least write yourself a to-do list on an index card, and carry it around with you. Buy a good three-year planning calendar. See pages 85–86 for information about such a calendar.

If you're a super-organized type, you're still not free from peril. You may be tempted to spend too much time sorting your files, and consequently miss out on genuine ministry. (See Paperwork.)

# Pacing

To correctly pace an event is to know when to start, when to have a break, and when to end. It's knowing how much to try to accomplish during the event.

Good pacing results in meaningful involvement and interest. Bad pacing loses or bores kids and creates the potential for problems with restlessness. Having a meeting right after lunch is bad pacing—unless the purpose of the meeting is a siesta.

A good rule of thumb is to end your meeting, game, or activity *before* anyone starts to look bored. This way you have them screaming for more, rather than having the activity sputter to a close. (See Timing.)

# Paperwork

Paperwork is part of youth work. You can't avoid forms, reimbursement receipts, letter writing, and mail-outs. You can see how paperwork can be a trap.

A computer can make your job easier, but never forget this: your job is people. Do only as much paperwork as it takes to do a good job with people work. Forget the rest. No one is likely to make a

**53**

posthumous book of your life, so don't bother giving them a paper archive to sort through. (See Files, Organization.)

# Parents

Almost every kid has at least one, sometimes four or five. If you can work with parents without abdicating control of your ministry, you've mastered a significant balancing act.

Avoid getting "between blood"—that is, taking sides in situations between parents and children, brothers and sisters, a boy and his dog. It's a no-win proposition.

# Pastors

Be your pastor's ambassador. Resist the temptation to join others in the widespread Christian pastime of snacking on roasted minister. Pray for your pastor. Meet with and inform your pastor of all the good stuff that's happening.

# Pencil Boxes

Create a box that can hold all the stuff you normally need for a meeting's paper-and-pencil activities: sharp pencils, erasers, tape, felt pens, glue, index cards, scissors, poster paper, and the like.

Like the jet stream in the upper atmosphere, like the currents in the ocean, there's a thing called *church drift*. Unless you put all your supplies in one secure location, they'll drift out of sight, out of usefulness, out of memory. So keep your stuff together so you can haul it with you to another room or to camp on a moment's notice. (See Prop Box.)

# Phone Chains

Most kids love to gab on the phone. So get their help creating a phone chain that will speed communication throughout your group. With a phone chain, you call a few kids and then they spread the word to the rest of the youth group through a network of phone calls.

# Photos

Take lots of photos of your kids. Drop them into your newsletters. You can get huge enlargements for cheap—see pages 85–86 for a source. Mount them and hang them around the church. Kids love to see themselves and relive the fun they've had.

# Points

Points are used to tabulate team scores during games or events. Since points are free, you can inflate them to any outrageous amount you like. Scoring 1,000 points—or even 100,000 points—sounds way more exciting to the average player than scoring one crummy point. Kids will work harder to get those tons of points because they're worth a lot more in their adolescent minds. It's one of those weird facts of youth work. (See Choosing Teams. Games.)

# Politics

Politics is everywhere. Even in churches you find politics—power, ambition, ego—coloring the scene. While living amid politics, you can at least learn to flex and compromise in order to avoid unpleasant situations. Be industrious rather than ambitious.

# Prayer

Pray for your kids regularly. Let them know you're praying for them. It stuns kids to hear someone say that they've been praying for them personally and regularly. It sets a good example, too.

# Preparation

Avoid flying by the seat of your pants. Prepare your lessons, materials, your room environment, and any other details well in advance of your students' arrivals. It will give you an air of authority and control and save on ulcer medicine. (See On Time.)

# Previewing

Insist on hearing a demo tape of any artist who wants to perform for your kids. Or do your homework by taking in one of his concerts. Otherwise, imagine the reactions of your teens when they show up for Christian Concert Nite only to hear your pastor's favorite—and highly recommended—

group, the Steadfast Anchor Gospel Yodelers.

View videos before showing them to your kids. Always see a film before hauling everyone off to see it (especially if it's PG-13 or worse). Always listen to tapes of speakers before you invite them to appear before your group.

The only exception is if the speaker, music, or video is recommended by someone who knows your kids and whose judgment you trust completely.

## Priorities

Youth work can be a never-ending job. A self-driven person can find endless jobs to be done. Without balance and a strong commitment to godly priorities, either you'll burn out or invite other personal disasters.

First on the priority list is a strong, intimate relationship with Christ. Second is healthy, accountable relationships (to a spouse if you're married, and to children if you have them). Keeping first things first will help you stay bright over the long haul and prevent you from ending up as a shooting star.

## Programs

A program isn't necessarily a ministry. Protect yourself from commitments that don't contribute directly to the direction you want the youth group to go. Don't be lassoed into leading the bell choir if the only bells your students play are fire alarms.

## Progression

Design your programs and activities to build upward. Seventh graders should have something to look forward to as they move into eighth. Activities should be different and get more exciting the older kids get. Hold back some activities from younger kids. A little yearning, a little waiting is good for them (and your program).

## Prop Boxes

Many meetings and events need props: paper and pencils, ropes, balls, board games, rubber chickens, double-sided coins for winning any argument, squirt guns, etc., etc. Running around town to find these goodies can take all day and cost money. So create a box where you can store all the little doodads you might need. Put each item in a zip lock bag, place the bags in the storage box, list the contents on a piece of paper, and tape the list to the outside of the box. Every year or so reorganize your prop box and revise the content list.

## Questionnaires

Hand out questionnaires to your kids from time to time. Their responses can help you find out a bunch of things in a hurry—who has the worst smelling feet, how many still sleep with a teddy bear, stuff like that.

You can also find out important stuff. Most kids enjoy spilling the beans about themselves on a questionnaire, especially an anonymous one. It makes them feel like their ideas and opinions count. See pages 85–86 for resources.

# Records

Keep records about your youth ministry.

Keep track of your regular meetings—teaching topic, date, audience, response. This way you'll be able to tell if you've taught Jesus Walking on the Water fourteen times in the last two months.

Keep track of special events, outings, and activities. Record the location, cost, number of kids involved, and any comments that will be helpful—in case you want to either repeat an event or avoid it at all costs.

Keep track of kids you meet individually or in small groups, and the nature of your meetings.

These notes, whether in hanging files or on your hard drive, are footprints to help you recall what you've done, what you've taught. The people who hired you may want the past year's accounting, too—and you'll have it all at hand.

# Recycling

Since kids cycle through your youth group in three or four years (most high schools being composed of three or four grades), you can probably recycle your program themes and events every four years.

If you do your own camps and retreats, for instance, you can drag out of your files a lot of the same material, publicity, games, and props every three or four years. This way you can use your energy and imagination to add to the theme or event instead of reinventing everything each time.

Of course, this idea doesn't work if your average tenure is a couple years. Long-haul folks only, thank you.

# Relevance

The symbolism behind the building materials of Solomon's temple may not have a ton of relevance to, say, your junior high boys. Relevance is helping kids see where biblical truth speaks to their everyday lives.

Relevance means understanding the world your kids live in. If it comes down to a choice, teach students the Scriptures they *need* to know rather than those they *ought* to know.

# Resources

Fortunately, there are huge amounts of books, curricula, teaching aids, music, and videos available to any youth worker who has the cash to pay for them. Start accumulating a youth ministry resource library of practical stuff. And don't loan any of it out—you'll probably need it a few hours later. Besides, if you loan it out, you'll never see it again anyway.

Resources don't mean you won't have to think or be creative. They just mean you'll have more raw materials to work with. See pages 85—86 for a list.

# Responsibilities

Never accept responsibility without an equal amount of authority. If you've been suckered into running the junior high department, for instance, you need to have a say in what direction the program is headed, what teaching materials will be used, and so on.

# Retention

Retention is what you remember of Sunday's sermon by dinner time. Not much, huh? A truth isn't learned well until it's retained. Do stuff that increases the retention level of your kids. Tell goofy stories, give them outrageous object lessons, take them places, get them personally involved in the lesson.

# Rites of Passage

Create separate rite-of-passage events for the younger teens in your group—one for the boys, another for the girls. We've done monster backpack treks, river rafting, cliff jumping—any kind of outing where endurance and courage are factors. You can use the event to talk to the kids about the attributes of God's man or woman—integrity, godliness, dependability, and so forth.

# Romances

Romance blossoms regularly in a youth group. Be aware of who's pairing off with whom, and set the standards for behavior in advance of cupid's strike. A few simple rules—no public displays of affection (the infamous PDAs), no guys in the gals' cabins, no gals in the guys' cabins—can cool off fiery hormones.

    If nighttime rendezvous are a problem during camps or

overnighters, you can create your own Cool-Off Squad by rounding up the hopelessly single guys in your group and arming them with Super Soakers filled with ice water, nylon stockings to pull over their faces, and permission to hose down any couple they find hiding in the woods.

# Rubber Chickens

Good youth workers have rubber chickens. The *best* youth workers have dozens of them. Uses are plentiful. They're usually served at most youth worker banquets as the main course.

# Rules

Gotta have rules. Just keep 'em simple, easy to understand, and broad enough to cover a multitude of sins. Don't tell a class, "No gum chewing, goofing off, spitting, shoving, swearing, or nose picking" when you can say instead, "You can't do anything that disturbs the learning of another student."

Never make a rule when you're tired or ticked off.

If your rules are going to be effective, they must be enforced—which mean they must be enforceable. So never tell a kid you'll throw him out of the van or leave him behind unless you're willing to do it. Never make a rule you won't or can't enforce. (See Brainwashing, Discipline.)

# Sacred Cows

Many churches have sacred cows—those places or items that can't be touched except by the right person at the right time. Take pew hurdling in the million-dollar sanctuary; this may not be the best idea for Youth Nite.

Learn what the sacred cows are and keep your kids away from them. You'll add longevity to your job.

# Salary

Circle the answer most appropriate to your current frame of mind:

a. Your salary is never enough.

b. Consider yourself lucky for getting paid to play.

c. At least you now know what to negotiate for at your *next* job.

# Seating

Kids want front-row seats at rock concerts, not at youth group.

Rear rows are typically considered choice seating. Yet if you control the seating, you can get kids more involved and probably circumvent problems that come from the back-row crew. Throw them some curve balls: assign seating with tickets and numbers. Or let the rear row fill up—and then when you're about to begin, have everyone turn their chairs around and make the back row the front row. Or start the meeting with fewer chairs than you'll need, and have helpers set up another back row or two of folding chairs only after the front rows have filled up.

# Self-Starters
It's necessary to be a true self-starter to be effective in youth ministry. Waiting around to be told what to do or doing only what's written on the job description spells a lackluster ministry. Youth work requires assertiveness and the ability to make the most of time, energy, and rubber chickens.

# Separation
Dividing and separating your group can be a good idea for both growth and effectiveness. Separate the junior highers from the senior highers, even if it means more work. (After all, they're not even the same species.) Separate guys from girls, especially if you want the guys to acknowledge any kind of personal weakness or need. It's an exercise in futility to expect a group of normal guys to admit being anything less than James Bond in front of even one girl.

# Sex
Most kids discover it while part of the youth group. It's your job to encourage them to leave the discovery alone. (See Romances.)

S S

# Showers of Blessings

Here's a novel clean-up idea for anyone who's had to shovel trash out of the church van after a trip.

When dropping off some kid, pull up in the driveway and simply say "Showers of blessings!" to the remaining occupants of the vehicle. This is their signal to throw all the van trash onto the

kid's lawn. Laugh and drive off. Just don't bless the same kid time after time; give everyone a chance to clean the van.

Doing this with the church *bus*, though, may make you highly unpopular with the one being blessed.

# Sorrow

Woe to the youth worker who makes a mistake and doesn't admit it. Usually everyone will know who left the church photocopier on all night with a rubber chicken hanging out of it. Confession and penance score points for your ministry.

# Spares

You know the feeling. Big Parent Night event when you absolutely need the overhead projector, and the bulb burns out during the second transparency. You gotta have a Band-Aid, but the first-aid kit is empty. The ball is flat, and the pump needle is missing. Keep handy spares of items that are likely to break, blow out, or be lost just when you need them.

# Spiritual Growth

The kid that grows the fastest doesn't necessarily grow the deepest. Don't overlook the kid who grows slowly but steadily.

# Staff

As your group grows, you'll need help from others. We call these folks *youth staff*. Figure on one volunteer staff person for every eight to ten kids, particularly in a class situation.

Let your staff know what you expect them to do. Train them to sit with kids and to get to know them. Teach them to spot the kids Nitro and Glycerin (every group has them) and to plop down between them so there won't be an explosion.

# Success

Success in youth work is no accident or stroke of luck. Success is directly related to work. Granted, hard work doesn't guarantee success, but it'll never be yours without work. Long weeks, long days, and long hours—usually for little pay—are part of the package. And there's not even a union to join.

To be a success in youth work does not mean that you're writing books, traveling the seminar circuit, or having a thousand kids turn up for your youth group. Success means that you've been able to walk with some kids during their adolescence and that by doing so they have a deeper relationship with Christ.

Of course, it won't hurt your pride of accomplishment if one of your kids winds up President of the United States.

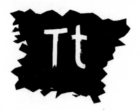

# Targeting

The personalities that form your youth group make all the difference in the world—specifically, the difference between growth and stagnation. Some groups are packed with listless kids; others have animated, energetic kids.

Targeting means setting your sights on the kind of kids that you want to have in your youth group, while at the same time working with the kids you have. Many sharp kids are already deeply committed to other activities. For kids to be willing to redirect their commitments, you'll have to present a faith that's worth the effort.

# Teachable Moments

Always be on the look-out for those teachable moments that occur in everyday life, for in these are the lessons that'll stick. If a young person dies whom your group knows, that's when talk about mortality and eternal life gets a ready audience. Don't be afraid to chuck the planned program to take advantage of teachable moments.

# Tension

Avoid the urge to explain everything to your students, or to have all the lessons wrapped up neatly. From time to time try teaching

like Jesus did. He'd tell a
strange story, then send
everyone home to figure
it out. Make your kids
work for answers. Leave
them arguing or debating
with each other. Create
situations where there's
tension—and then go
home. Kids will learn *how*
to think, not merely *what* to think.

## Thank-You Notes

Be a note writer. You'll keep your volunteer workers or involved
parents much longer if you pay them this courtesy for their efforts.

## Thinking Ahead

Run your youth group like you drive. Stay focused, look ahead.
Give yourself plenty of room to maneuver around the potholes,
since crises of one sort or another will inevitably be in your path.
And keep one eye on your gas gauge—take whatever breaks you
need to avoid burnout.

## Time

Start on time, end on time, leave on time. Leave behind kids who
are not on time (after a five-minute grace period to compensate
for watches that might be off a bit). Do this once or twice and
everyone will be on time. You'll get a cool reputation, too.

If you want to attract attention to your meeting, start at a
weird time—like 7:21 p.m.

About ending your message on time: inexperienced speakers finish their messages, no matter what the clock is saying. Yet it's better to end on time and leave the group wanting more than to bore them with too much. (See On Time, Timing.)

# Timing

The schedules of kids in your area run according to cycles. Figure the cycles out, then use the knowledge to your advantage. Are two-thirds of the kids gone during August? Do many of them get jobs at Christmas break? Then August and December are lousy times to throw a big event. There's nothing worse than renting the stadium and having eight kids show up. But August and December *may* be good times to work with small groups.

Figure out your group's cycle, and plan accordingly. (See On Time, Time.)

# Tools

Every youth worker's quiver should contain these arrows:
➤ A shelf full of helpful books
➤ Two cameras: a 35mm and a vidcam
➤ A computer with publishing software
➤ A top-quality rubber chicken
(See Video Gear.)

# Toy Stores

Prowl toy stores from time to time. Look for some new gadget or idea you can work into your fun-and-game events.

# Trophies

Kids are still suckers for trophies and certificates. You can make some off-the-wall trophies cheaply with creative combinations of empty cans, small plastic toys or gimmick items, squares of wood, and spray paint. Hold it all together with silicon glue.

If you have the right software (which is usually inexpensive), computers can spit out terrific certificates. They're cheap to generate, so use them liberally! Give framed certificates to the kid who snores loudest at camp, to the best actors in your video production, to the most helpful members of your group. Give them for anything that deserves recognition.

# Troublemakers

Most troublemakers are really leaders leading in the wrong direction. At a new job, find out quickly which kids might be labeled as troublemakers. Make an attempt to get to know them and win them to your side. Some of the best leaders in the Bible were considered big troublemakers by almost everyone else.

# Ubiquity

You can't be every place all the time, though you're expected to be. If something goes wrong during your watch, the buck stops with you.

Resist the temptation to kick back with a couple of your favorite kids while the rest of the crew is terrorizing the neighborhood. From beginning to end, your duty is to know what the whole group is doing.

If you have an especially large or rowdy group, your strategy should be assigning helpers to watch various locations or keep track of particular kids who tend to slip away or get out of hand. Yes, you need baby-sitters.

# Ugly Ducklings

Most youth groups have one or two kids who fit this description. You may not be able to prevent the cruelty of kids trying to carve up an outcast, but you can help the ugly duckling feel like a swan—which is, by the way, a special privilege for youth workers. Make a place for the ugly ducklings.

# Unassailability

A good ministry can be taken down by rumors and innuendoes. They don't have to be true to be disaster. Protect yourself from those who revel in bringing down a godly man or woman.

➤ When dropping kids off, make sure the last student you drop off is the same gender as you, even if it means going out of your way.

➤ Guard yourself from being too touchy-feely with kids. While it may seem harmless to you, you can raise the eyebrows of others and create improper feelings in some needy kids.

➤ If you're married, invest your intimacy with your spouse, not with a coworker.

➤ Keep your rubber chicken away from roosters.

➤ Don't you (or your interns or staff) date kids in the youth group.

➤ Be cautious handling money. Have someone with you when you count funds collected from events.

# Video Gear

By all means invest in a vidcam, editing equipment and—if possible—a video projector. If you have no skill or interest in this medium, then find kids who do. (Lots do.) Don't let kids fool you when they scream, "Oh, no! Don't show any pictures of me!" They have huge egos and love to see themselves on the screen.

# Vintage

Like a fine wine, youth workers get better with age. You may get slower, but you make up for it by getting smarter. Youth work isn't a profession for only the young; it can be a lifelong career.

Being youth workers, of course, we have no idea what a fine wine tastes like.

# Vocal Minorities

It's often a vocal minority that calls the shots in youth groups (and in churches as well). It pays to know who to listen to when you want key information. You may discover that the vocal minority are the very ones *not* to listen to.

# Weird Stuff

Kids love weird stuff. An event starting at 1 a.m. is weird. A mystery menu that gives kids no idea what they're ordering is weird. An invitation or mailout in code or puzzle pieces is kind of weird. A rubber chicken dangling from a kid's ceiling fan in the morning is weird squared. The more weird stuff you pull, the higher your fun-guy stock shoots up. Get weird.

# Writing

Get it in writing! Most problems in church are caused by miscommunication. When the words are down in black and white, no one can wiggle out with *I thought you said* or *You didn't tell me.*

# Xenophobia

Some youth groups are plagued with fear of foreigners. They're a closed circle, inbred, almost hostile to anyone coming into their midst. If you inherit a group like this, you may need to work around the chosen people to bring in new blood. (See Cliques, Inheritance.)

# Youth Leadership

Youth leadership—kids leading kids—comes in many flavors and varieties. Some groups hold mini-election campaigns...some have teams of volunteers that commit to service (our favorite method, because you get dedicated workers running the group, not merely the popular)...others use high school seniors to plan for the rest of the group (a good idea, because it gives rank and responsibility to age).

The key is to allow kids to have input and ownership, though without the final say about what goes on. You're the youth worker, so you reserve the right of veto over any student-leadership group. Otherwise you may end up explaining why the kids are bungee jumping from the church steeple.

Kids typically have a limited number of programming ideas; most of the time they want a rerun of the last great activity. They'll need your input. Try to give suggestions to the leadership group casually, so they think it's really their idea. This works with kids, of course, because you're smarter than they are. And they know it.

# Youth Workers

You are a Youth Worker. Repeat that five times. It'll help.

(You may be a Professional Youth Worker. The difference between a professional youth worker and a lay youth worker is that the professional has managed to con someone into coughing up a salary.)

Most youth workers are seen as a bit strange. People may roll their eyes when they introduce you. It's understandable—most professions don't come with offices filled with toys, most notably rubber chickens.

Age, looks, or hipness does not make a youth worker. Love and concern for kids, coupled with a degree of relational ability, does.

## Zero Money

On occasion a church has little or no funds to run a youth program. You'll need to create your own income and budget.

Youth projects can raise some funds. Inform the kids that they need to help carry their own weight. Chances are, most can fill a youth offering basket with more than straw wrappers and nickels. Many parents, when properly presented with the necessities of youth work, will give generously. (See Fundraising.)

## Zits

Acne—and B.O. , dandruff, bad breath, stinky feet, and sudden weird changes to the body—are all part of the scenery for teenagers. Don't assume that your kids know the joys of deodorant, dandruff shampoo, Odor Eaters, or acne pads. Be a friend—tell them directly and privately. Those sitting nearby will thank you for it.

# STEP RIGHT UP
# AND GET YOUR RESOURCES

**Really huge photos for cheap** (see page 55)
York Photo Lab
400 Rayon Dr.
Parkersburg, WV 26101
304/424-9675

**Design 'em yourself book covers** (see page 10)
Walraven Book Cover Company
P.O. Box 830609
Richardson, TX 75083-0609
214/235-1281

**Three-year calendars** (see page 52)
Calendars
P.O. Box 400
Sidney, NY 13838
607/563-7337
fax 607/563-8811

**Magazines for your students**
➤ *Campus Life* 800/678-6083
➤ *You!* 818/991-1813
➤ *Insight* 800/765-6955

**Fun & games**
➤ *Play It* and *Play It Again*, Wayne Rice and Mike Yaconelli (Youth Specialties)
➤ *Ideas* Library, (Youth Specialties)
➤ *Quick Crowdbreakers and Games for Youth Groups*, (Group Publishing)

**Retreats & camps**
➤ *Great Retreats for Youth Groups*, Chris Cannon (Youth Specialties)
➤ "1997 Retreat, Trip, and Travel Guide" *Group Magazine*, January 1997 Issue

## Teaching
➤ *Talksheets*, David Lynn (Youth Specialties)
➤ *Hot Illustrations for Youth Workers Books 1 & 2*, Wayne Rice (Youth Specialties)
➤ *Incredible Questionnaires for Youth Ministry*, Rick Bundschuh and E.G. Von Trutzschler (Youth Specialties)
➤ *Outrageous Object Lessons*, E.G. Von Trutzschler (Gospel Light Publications)
➤ *Kickstarters: 101 Ingenious Intros to Just about Any Bible Lesson*, Rick Bundschuh and Tom Finley (Youth Specialties)

## Fundraising
➤ *Great Fundraising Ideas for Youth Groups* and *More Great Fundraising Ideas for Youth Groups*, David Lynn and Kathy Lynn (Youth Specialties)

## Reference
➤ *Dictionary of Cults, Sects, Religions, and the Occult*, George A. Mather and Larry A. Nichols (Zondervan)

## Major curriculum publishers

David C. Cook/Scripture Press
4050 Lee Vance View
Colorado Springs, CO 80918
719/536-0100

Gospel Light Publications
2300 Knoll Dr.
Ventura CA 93003
800/235-3415

Group Publishing
Box 481
Loveland, CO 80539
970/669-3836

Standard Publishing
8121 Hamilton Ave.
Cincinnati, OH 45231
800/543-1301

Youth Specialties
1224 Greenfield Dr.
El Cajon, CA 92021
619/440-2333
Orders: 800/776-8008

# YOUTH SPECIALTIES TITLES

## Professional Resources

Administration, Publicity, & Fundraising (Ideas Library)
Developing Student Leaders
Equipped to Serve: Volunteer Youth Worker Training Course
Help! I'm a Junior High Youth Worker!
Help! I'm a Small-Group Leader!
Help! I'm a Sunday School Teacher!
Help! I'm a Volunteer Youth Worker!
How to Expand Your Youth Ministry
How to Speak to Youth...and Keep Them Awake at the Same Time
Junior High Ministry (Updated & Expanded)
The Ministry of Nurture: A Youth Worker's Guide to Discipling Teenagers
One Kid at a Time: Reaching Youth through Mentoring
Purpose-Driven Youth Ministry
So That's Why I Keep Doing This! 52 Devotional Stories for Youth Workers
A Youth Ministry Crash Course
The Youth Worker's Handbook to Family Ministry

## Youth Ministry Programming

Camps, Retreats, Missions, & Service Ideas (Ideas Library)
Compassionate Kids: Practical Ways to Involve Your Students in Mission and Service
Creative Bible Lessons from the Old Testament
Creative Bible Lessons in 1 & 2 Corinthians
Creative Bible Lessons in John: Encounters with Jesus
Creative Bible Lessons in Romans: Faith on Fire!
Creative Bible Lessons on the Life of Christ
Creative Junior High Programs from A to Z, Vol. 1 (A-M)
Creative Junior High Programs from A to Z, Vol. 2 (N-Z)
Creative Meetings, Bible Lessons, & Worship Ideas (Ideas Library)

Crowd Breakers & Mixers (Ideas Library)
Drama, Skits, & Sketches (Ideas Library)
Drama, Skits, & Sketches 2 (Ideas Library)
Dramatic Pauses
Everyday Object Lessons
Games (Ideas Library)
Games 2 (Ideas Library)
Great Fundraising Ideas for Youth Groups
More Great Fundraising Ideas for Youth Groups
Great Retreats for Youth Groups
Greatest Skits on Earth
Greatest Skits on Earth, Vol. 2
Holiday Ideas (Ideas Library)
Hot Illustrations for Youth Talks
More Hot Illustrations for Youth Talks
Still More Hot Illustrations for Youth Talks
Incredible Questionnaires for Youth Ministry
Junior High Game Nights
More Junior High Game Nights
Kickstarters: 101 Ingenious Intros to Just about Any Bible Lesson
Live the Life! Student Evangelism Training Kit
Memory Makers
Play It! Great Games for Groups
Play It Again! More Great Games for Groups
Special Events (Ideas Library)
Spontaneous Melodramas
Super Sketches for Youth Ministry
Teaching the Bible Creatively
Videos That Teach
What Would Jesus Do? Youth Leader's Kit
The Next Level
Wild Truth Bible Lessons
Wild Truth Bible Lessons 2
Wild Truth Bible Lessons— Pictures of God
Worship Services for Youth Groups

## Discussion Starters

Discussion & Lesson Starters (Ideas Library)
Discussion & Lesson Starters 2 (Ideas Library)

Get 'Em Talking
Keep 'Em Talking!
High School TalkSheets
More High School TalkSheets
High School TalkSheets: Psalms and Proverbs
Junior High TalkSheets
More Junior High TalkSheets
Junior High TalkSheets: Psalms and Proverbs
What If...? 450 Thought Provoking Questions to Get Teenagers Talking, Laughing, and Thinking
Would You Rather...? 465 Provocative Questions to Get Teenagers Talking
Have You Ever...? 450 Intriguing Questions Guaranteed to Get Teenagers Talking

## Clip Art

ArtSource: Stark Raving Clip Art (print)
ArtSource: Youth Group Activities (print)
ArtSource CD-ROM: Clip Art Library Version 2.0

## Videos

EdgeTV
The Heart of Youth Ministry: A Morning with Mike Yaconelli
Next Time I Fall in Love Video Curriculum
Purpose Driven Youth Ministry Video Curriculum
Understanding Your Teenager Video Curriculum

## Student Books

Grow For It Journal
Grow For It Journal through the Scriptures
Teen Devotional Bible
What Would Jesus Do? Spiritual Challenge Journal
Spiritual Challenge Journal: The Next Level
Wild Truth Journal for Junior Highers
Wild Truth Journal—Pictures of God